Anonymous

Lexington

A handbook of its points of interest, historical and picturesque

Anonymous

Lexington
A handbook of its points of interest, historical and picturesque

ISBN/EAN: 9783337221461

Printed in Europe, USA, Canada, Australia, Japan

Cover: Foto ©ninafisch / pixelio.de

More available books at **www.hansebooks.com**

LEXINGTON.

A

HAND-BOOK

OF ITS

POINTS OF INTEREST,

HISTORICAL AND PICTURESQUE.

PUBLISHED UNDER THE DIRECTION OF THE LEXINGTON
HISTORICAL SOCIETY.

1891.

For Sale by
W. B. CLARKE & CO.
340 Washington Street,
BOSTON, MASS.

PRESS OF CARL H. HEINTZEMANN. HALF-TONES BY LEWIS ENG. CO.

Copies of the original photographs (size, 9 ins. x 7 ins.) of the pictures on pages 6, 7, 8, 10, 12, 14, 15, 16, 19, 20, 21, 22, 23, 24, 28, 29, 32, 35, 37, 38, 40, 41, 42, 43, 45, 46, 48, 49, 50, 53, 57, 58, 59, 60, 70, may be obtained (mounted) at the following prices (postpaid): —

Single copies	$ .50
6 copies (one view)	2.50
6 copies (different views)	2.75
12 copies (one view)	4.50
12 copies (different views)	5.00
Historical set (15 views)	6.00
Complete set (35 views)	13.00

Orders to be sent to

GUIDE-BOOK COMMITTEE,

P.O. Box 65,

Lexington, Mass.

CONTENTS.

	PAGE.
INDEX .	73
MAP .	4

TOPOGRAPHY	5
HISTORY . . .	6
LEXINGTON COMMON . .	12
Meeting House Monument	13
Grant Elm . .	13
Buckman Tavern	14
Line of Battle	14
Harrington House .	15
Monument .	16
Munroe House	18
Belfry . .	18
Burying Ground	19
Hancock Church .	21
Hancock-Clarke House	22
LINE OF THE BRITISH ADVANCE AND RETREAT . .	27
HISTORICAL TABLETS AND MONUMENTS ALONG THE LINE	31
Jonathan Harrington House . . .	31
Munroe Tavern	32
Sanderson House	32
Cannon Tablets	33
Merriam House	34
Hayward Tablet	34
OTHER POINTS OF INTEREST	35
Parker Homestead	35
Cary Farm	36
Grapevine Corner	38
Waltham St	38
Main St . . .	40

Contents.

	PAGE.
East Lexington	42
Southerly Lexington	44
Hancock St	47
North Lexington	51
Merriam's Hill	52
Concord Hill	54
PUBLIC BUILDINGS	57
Hancock School House	57
Town Hall	57
Cary Library	58
Memorial Hall	59
Savings Bank	59
High School House	60
Village Hall	60
Adams School House	60
Manufactures	61
Churches, Societies, etc	61
DRIVES	64
WALKS	70
CHURCH SERVICES	71
POST OFFICES	72
CARY LIBRARY—HOURS	72
INDEX	73

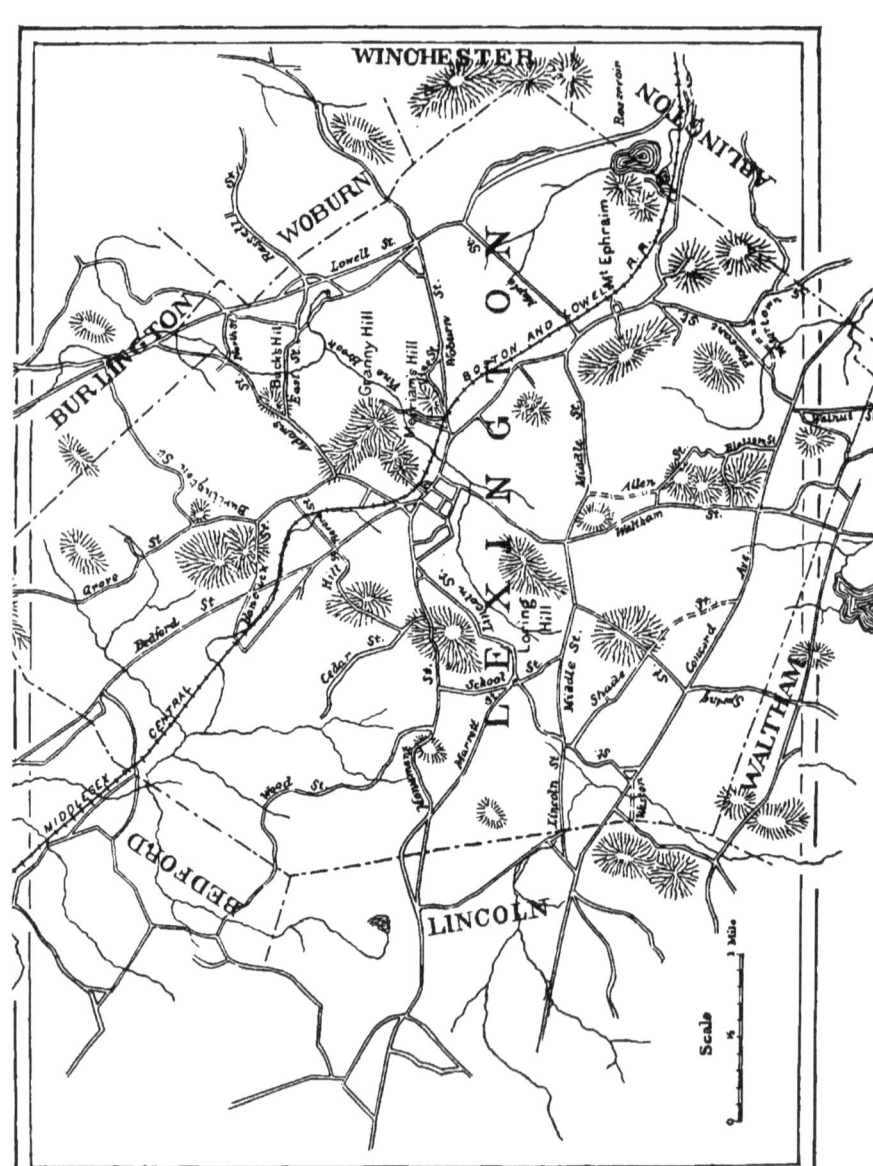

LEXINGTON.

LEXINGTON lies northwest of Boston, at a distance of ten miles. It is reached by train from the Southern Division Station of the Boston and Maine R. R., on Causeway St., passing through Cambridge, Somerville, and Arlington. The railroad accommodations are excellent, twenty-two trains running daily each way.[1]

The town has an extent of territory of about 12,000 acres. It adjoins Bedford and Burlington on the north, Woburn, Winchester and Arlington on the east, Belmont and Waltham on the south, and Lincoln on the west. According to the last census the population numbers 3,200, and the property valuation of the town amounts to about $3,500,000.

Farming is the principal occupation of the inhabitants, and the chief productions are hay, milk, fruit and vegetables. Many business men of Boston have residences here, and during the summer and autumn Lexington is a favorite resort. The location is peculiarly favorable to health, and invalids find the bracing air and pure water very beneficial. Being nearly 250 feet higher than sea level, it forms the water-shed between the Charles River on the south, the Concord on the north, and the Mystic on the east.

There are no stagnant ponds within its borders, and brooks run from it in almost every direction. The surface is greatly diversified, abounding in hills of considerable height which afford extensive views over the adjoining towns. From many points the Wachusett and Monadnock Mountains are plainly seen in the western horizon. Containing many large, well-tilled farms, pleasant dwellings with fine old trees around them, and extensive tracts of woodland, the drives over its sixty miles of roads are picturesque and delightful.

---

[1] A single fare to Lexington Centre is twenty-two cents, and a hundred-ride ticket may be purchased for $12.50.

HISTORY.

Lexington probably derived its name from Lord Lexington, a British statesman of some prominence in the early part of the eighteenth century, when the town was incorporated. It was originally a part of Cambridge, and was set apart as a parish in December, 1692, by act of the

BUCKMAN TAVERN.

General Court, under the name of "Cambridge Farms." Large grants of land were made to Cambridge people as early as 1637, on condition that they should clear the land, erect buildings thereon, and make it their place of residence.

History.

The first clearing was made in the vicinity of Vine Brook, in what is now the central village, and a house built by Robert Herlarkenden, about 1640. This was probably near the site of the present Merriam house, formerly known as the Buckman Tavern (*See p. 14*). After the organization of the parish in 1692, a meeting-house was erected at the junction of what are now Bedford and Monument Sts., and Benjamin Estabrook was employed to preach, but the church was not organized until four years later, when he was ordained and settled as the minister of the parish. In the following year, 1697, Mr. Estabrook died and was succeeded by Rev. John Hancock, who remained the pastor until his death in 1752, after a settlement of fifty-five years. He was the grandfather of John Hancock, President of the first Continental Congress, and the first governor of Massachusetts.

MEETING-HOUSE MONUMENT.

In 1713, the parish was set off from Cambridge and incorporated as a town, with the name of Lexington. In the same year a new meeting-house was built near the old one, on land bought of "Nibour Muzzy" for a Common. It was fifty feet in length by forty feet in width, and twenty-eight feet in height. Having no steeple, the bell was hung in a belfry placed near it, and the bell appears to have been given to the town by Cambridge. This meeting-house and the belfry (*See p. 18.*) are seen in all pictures of the battle of Lexington. In 1715, the first schoolhouse was built; this also was placed on the Common, and occupied the site where the old monument now stands,

BELFRY.

afterwards known as "Schoolhouse Hill." A grammar school was established after its completion and taught for many years by Capt. Joseph Estabrook, the first schoolmaster of Lexington. It was not a free school, however, each pupil being obliged "to pay two pens per week for reading, and three pens for righting and siphering." It was opened only to boys at first, but subsequently the town voted to admit "gairls." In the same year "dame schools," which were free to all, were established in the "out-skirts" and were taught by women, in rooms of private houses.

At an early day the town was noted for its military spirit, and furnished its full share of soldiers for the Indian and French wars. When trouble with the mother country arose and affairs became critical, the people were prompt to organize for resistance to all encroachment upon their rights.

FIRST SCHOOL-HOUSE. — 1715.

A company of minute-men was formed, numbering one hundred and twenty, under the command of Capt. John Parker. Probably it embraced all able-bodied men capable of bearing arms in town. This company was steadily drilling for some time before the beginning of the conflict, and the town kept a stock of powder stored in the upper gallery of the meeting-house, with balls, flints, etc. Thus, long before a blow was struck or the idea of independence seriously entertained, Lexington was preparing for the conflict. On the ever memorable 19th of April, 1775, this company of fearless patriots received, on Lexington Common, the first shock of battle, and before the day closed ten of their number had sealed their devotion to the cause with their

10   *Lexington.*

HANCOCK SCHOOL-HOUSE. — 1891.

lives, and nine were wounded, a larger loss than that of any other town. During the war of the Revolution, Lexington was represented in seventeen different campaigns, and many of her sons perished on distant battle-fields. One hundred and seven men from the town enlisted for three years, or during the war, and a larger number for shorter terms of service. When we remember that the whole population did not exceed 800, it will be seen that the town was not wanting in devotion to the cause of American Independence. During the war of the Rebellion, the same patriotic spirit animated her citizens. Nearly 200 men were sent into the service by this town, of whom fourteen died, while in the army, from wounds or sickness. At the close of the war, Lexington had her quota more than full, and had expended $30,000 for the soldiers and their families. Thus the town has an honorable record of sacrifice and service in the cause of national independence and of freedom. (*See p. 59.*)

THE COMMON — LOOKING NORTH.

LEXINGTON COMMON.

The most interesting spot in the town to its people and to visitors is the Common. This is a small plat of ground in the central village, about two minutes' walk north of the central railroad station. It has the form of a triangle, and is bounded by Monument St., Bedford St. and Elm

Avenue. The purchase of an acre and a half of this ground was made in 1711, by a subscription of sixteen pounds. It was bought of "Nibour Muzzy" for public use. An additional acre was bought a few years later, for twenty-five pounds, to enlarge the Common toward the north, making two and one-half acres in all; an area which has been considerably reduced by cutting Bedford Street through the eastern side.

Meeting House Monument. At the southern point stands a monument marking the site of the first three meeting-houses erected in Lexington. It faces down Main St., and bears on the front an appro-

THIRD MEETING-HOUSE. — 1794-1846 — FROM BARBER'S HISTORICAL COLLECTIONS.

priate inscription, and on the rear the names of the first seven pastors of the parish, with the dates of their pastorates. A few feet in the rear of this monument, and enclosed by a wire netting, is the elm planted by President Grant at the Centennial of the battle, April 19th, 1875. (*See p. 7.*)

Lexington.

Buckman Tavern. On Bedford St., directly opposite this monument, is the Merriam house, known at the time of the battle as the Buckman Tavern. It was the rallying place of the minute-men on the night of April 18th, and on the morning of the encounter at the Common. It contains bullet holes made by the shots of British soldiers, who were fired upon from the house. In the small one-story L of this house was kept, for many years, the first post-office of Lexington. (*See p. 6*).

BOULDER.

Line of Battle. About ten rods north from the Meeting-house Monument is seen a large boulder, placed here to mark the line of the minute-men in the battle. An old musket with a powder-horn thrown over it is carved on the face and points the direction of the line. Underneath are inscribed the words used by Captain Parker to his men: "Stand your ground; don't fire unless fired upon; but if they mean to have a war, let it begin here."

This command is found in a letter of Rev. Theodore Parker, Capt. Parker's grandson (*See p. 35*), to George Bancroft, as a tradition held in the Parker family. It was confirmed by Col. William Munroe, the orderly sergeant of Capt. Parker's company, who formed the line of battle on April 19th, 1775. When the battle was acted out on the Common in 1822, Col. Munroe personated Capt. Parker and repeated these words, adding, "Them is the very words Captain Parker spoke." This boulder, it is estimated, weighs from twelve to fifteen tons, and was drawn to

HARRINGTON HOUSE.

the spot, from a distance of two miles, by a team of ten horses. It fitly symbolizes the firm, unyielding spirit of the men whose deed it commemorates.

Harrington House. On Elm Avenue, a few rods directly north of the boulder and fronting the Common, stands a venerable house occupied at the time of the battle by the family of Jonathan

16   Lexington.

Harrington. He belonged to Capt. Parker's company, and fell, mortally wounded by the British volley. A tablet on the house relates the fact that he dragged himself to the door and died at his wife's feet. This house was built by Dr. David Fiske (*See p. 50*), and was, at one time, the home of John Augustus (*See p. 20*). A giant elm stands before it.

MONUMENT. FIRST PARISH CHURCH IN BACKGROUND.

Monument. Turning to the west side of the Common, on a rounded knoll is seen the old monument, erected by the State in 1799. It is probably the oldest memorial of the Revolution in the country. It bears upon its face the names of the Lexington heroes who fell in the battle, with an elaborate inscription (*See p. 30*) written by Rev. Jonas Clarke, the minister of the town for half a century (*See p. 24*). In the rear of this monument is a stone vault which contains the remains of the martyrs to freedom, deposited there on the sixtieth anniversary of their death. The bodies of the slain were buried originally in the old cemetery and, after reposing there until 1835, were taken up and borne to the meeting-house, where an oration was pronounced by Edward Everett and, in the presence of a

MARRETT MUNROE HOUSE.

vast assemblage, the remains were laid, by their surviving comrades, in this final resting place.

In front of the old monument Lafayette was welcomed to Lexington in September, 1825. Here fourteen of Capt. Parker's minute-men were introduced to him, and the school children, marching by, scattered garlands at his feet. Here, also, Kossuth and many other distinguished persons have been received.

Munroe House. A little farther south on Monument St., facing the Common, is seen a slant-roofed house, built in 1729, and occupied at the time of the battle by Marrett Munroe. Towards this house Caleb Harrington was running from the meeting-house, where he had been to get powder, when he was shot by the British soldiers. A bullet from a British musket passed through the window over the door and lodged in a bureau, where it still remains, in the possession of one of Mr. Munroe's descendants living in Chicopee, Mass.

The Old Belfry. In 1761 a new bell was given to the town by Isaac Stone, and a belfry was erected for it on the hill, now called "Belfry Hill," a little to the south of the Munroe house. Here it remained for six years, when it was moved down to the Common and placed near where the old monument now stands. From this belfry was rung out the alarm on the morning of the 19th of April, 1775, calling the minute-men to assemble on the Common. It remained there for thirty years, summoning the people to worship, warning them at nine at night to rake up the fires and go to bed, and tolling for them when, one after another, they passed away. In 1797, it was purchased by the son of Capt. John Parker, removed to his homestead in the south part of the town (*See p. 35*), and used for a wheelwright's shop. There it stood for nearly a century, but recently it was given to the Lexington Historical Society and has been removed to Belfry Hill, not far from the spot where it was built one hundred and thirty years ago. It stands on the side of the hill just above the new school-house and is approached by way of Clarke and Forest Sts. Though much dilapidated, it has been restored to its original appearance and is cherished as a precious memento of the olden time (*See p. 8*). The bell has long since disappeared; but the tongue which rang out the first notes of American Independence has been rescued from destruction and is now preserved among the invaluable relics in the Cary Library (*See p. 58*).

The ancient Burying Ground. A short distance beyond the Unitarian Meeting-house, which faces the common, at the junction of Elm Avenue with Monument St., a lane leads to the old burying ground. It is a pleasant spot, having an outlook over the meadows along the North Brook, towards the eastern slope of Davis Hill. So far as known, it contains the oldest graves in the town; some of the stones bear the

MONUMENT TO CAPTAIN PARKER.

date of 1690, though probably many unmarked graves were made there much earlier. A monument to Capt. John Parker, commander of the minute-men, April 19th, 1775, was erected by the town in 1884, over the supposed site of his grave. It is a single block of granite, pyramidal in form, set upon a heavy base, and bears an appropriate inscription. Near it is the tomb of the Rev. Benjamin Estabrook, the first minister of Lexington, and, close by, the grave of his brother, Capt. Joseph, the first schoolmaster. An obelisk of white marble marks the burial place of Gov. William Eustis, one of the early governors of Massachusetts (1823-25), and a distinguished surgeon in the army of the Revolution. It was his request to be laid beside his mother,

EUSTIS MONUMENT.

who was at one time a resident of the town, and his own name appears on the roll of Captain Parker's company. In the vicinity of Governor Eustis's monument is the tomb of the Revs. John Hancock and Jonas Clarke and their families (*See p. 22*). It is covered by a large stone slab placed upon six pillars, and in the vault below, in addition to the remains of Mr. Hancock and of his wife, are those of their son, Rev. Ebenezer Hancock, those of Mr. and Mrs. Clarke, of Lucy Clarke, the wife of Dr. Henry Ware, of Mr. Clarke's son Bowen, and of his two unmarried daughters, Elizabeth and Sarah. The tomb was sealed up in 1843, when the last of Mr. Clarke's daughters was placed there. A curious monumental stone may be seen near the entrance to the burying ground, having inscribed upon it the names of six children belonging to one family, all of whom died within twelve days. (*See p. 22*). In one of the tombs near by are the remains of John Augustus, a resident of Lexington, who is remembered for his benevolent activity in Boston, half a century ago, in caring for juvenile offenders at the Municipal Court, rescuing many boys and girls from a career of crime. At the left of the entrance to the burying ground is an enclosure containing the graves of many members of the Merriam, Simonds, Robbins and Parker families. Here also is the grave of Rev. Caleb Stetson, for many years pastor of the Unitarian Church in Medford, together with that of his wife, Julia Merriam, a native of the town.

HANCOCK-CLARKE TOMB.

Passing up Elm Avenue to its junction with Hancock St., opposite the northeast corner of the Common, we come to the meeting-house of Hancock Church, a plain, unpretentious building, which has an interesting history. It was erected in 1822, for the use of Lexington Academy. But that institution becoming extinct in 1833, it was offered to the State by the town, in 1839, for the establishment of a normal school. The offer was accepted, and the school was opened here in July of that year with three pupils,

Hancock Church.

under the charge of Rev. Cyrus Pierce, familiarly known as "Father Pierce." This was the first normal school established in the United

States. After five years it was removed to West Newton, and subsequently to Framingham, where it is now permanently located.

The Hancock-Clarke House. On Hancock St., about a hundred rods north of the Common, stands the Hancock-Clarke House. The original portion of it is the one-story gambrel-roofed L, erected in 1698 or 1699, by Rev. John Hancock, the second minister. In this humble dwelling his five children, three sons and two daughters, were born. The eldest son, John, was graduated at Harvard and became the minister of Braintree, now Quincy, where his son John, of the Revolution, was born. The second son, Thomas, was apprenticed to a bookbinder in Boston, and,

FIRST NORMAL SCHOOL.—1839.

after serving out his time, went into business for himself and rose rapidly in wealth and influence until he became the richest merchant in New England. In 1734, he bought Beacon Hill, including the present site of the State House, and erected there the famous stone house known as the "Hancock Mansion." The third son, Ebenezer, was graduated at Harvard and became his father's colleague in the pastor-

HANCOCK-CLARKE HOUSE.

ate of the church, dying here in 1740. The daughters both married clergymen. Thomas Hancock built, in 1734, the two-storied addition to the original house, for the comfort of his father and mother, and here the old people died "full of years and honors." But a more eventful history remains to be told of the old house under the succeeding occupant and owner, Rev. Jonas Clarke, the fourth minister of Lexington. Marrying Lucy Bowes, a grand-daughter of his predecessor, in 1760, he bought the estate and lived there until his death in 1805. Here their thirteen children were born and grew up to manhood and womanhood; two of them remained in the house until they died, in 1843. Four of Mr. Clarke's daughters married ministers, and not

HANCOCK-CLARKE ELM.

less than twenty-five clergymen are either included among the descendants of John Hancock and Jonas Clarke, or were connected with them by marriage and are hence associated with this house. The ministry, in Lexington, of these two men covered a period of one hundred and five years. Young John Hancock was a cousin of Mrs. Clarke and a frequent visitor in the family. Much of his boyhood and youth had been passed here under the care of his grandfather, the aged minister. On the night of the 18th of April, 1775, in company with that staunch patriot, Samuel Adams, he was sleeping in the west room of the lower floor when aroused by Paul Revere. Under apprehension that an attempt would be made by Gen. Gage to arrest them, a guard of eight men had been stationed around the house for their protection. After giving the alarm, Revere returned to the Common and rode on towards Concord. Hancock and Adams were conducted to the house of Madam Jones, in Burlington, about four miles distant. But word coming that the British were on their track and close at hand, they were led to the house of Amos Wyman in Billerica, two miles farther away, where they remained during the day (*See Drive No. 17, p. 67*).

At the time of the battle the ground was all open between Mr. Clarke's house and the Common, and the firing was plainly seen from the chamber windows. As Mrs. Clarke and her children were leaving the yard for a more secure place, a bullet whizzed by and lodged in the barn, barely missing one of the daughters, who was carrying a baby in her arms. During the day Mr. Clarke remained at the house, and as the minute-men were going to and returning from the conflict, he offered them such refreshment as he possessed, until his bread, meat and cider were exhausted.

Jonas Clarke was an ardent patriot, heartily devoted to the cause of American liberty, and a wise counsellor, conversant with political affairs. His house became, naturally, the gathering place of patriots and statesmen before and during the Revolutionary period. Many literary men, college presidents and professors, governors of the state and men prominent in social and political life used to gather around his hospitable board and discuss the burning questions of the time. The venerable house is thus associated with many historic personages and events, and is an object of especial interest to all visitors to Lexington.

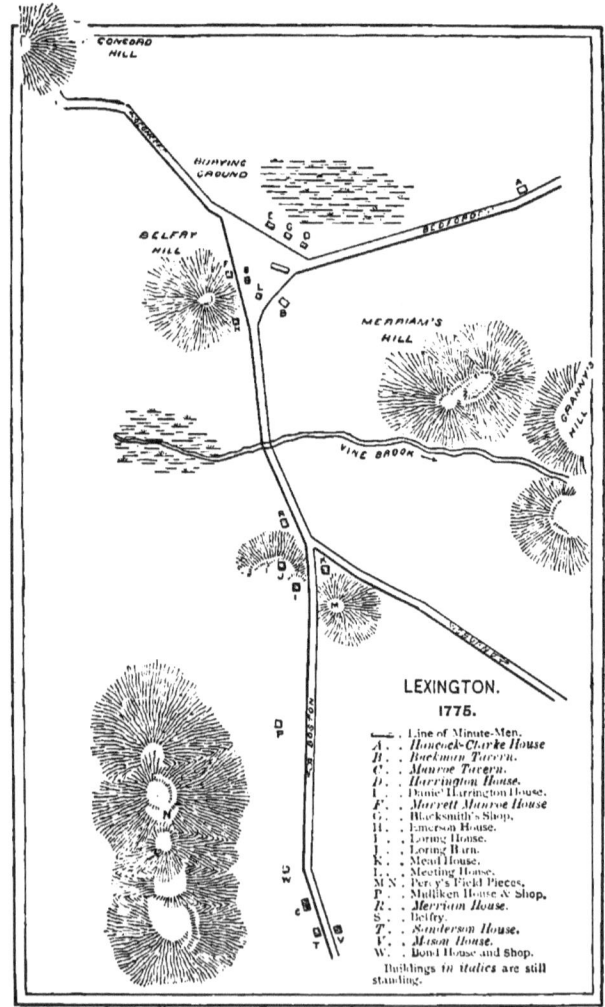

LINE OF THE BRITISH ADVANCE AND RETREAT.

Main St., extending from the Arlington line, on the southeast, to the Common, has substantially the same location now as in 1775. This was the route of the British troops on the morning of the 19th of April, when they came to Lexington to arrest Hancock and Adams, and marched on to Concord to destroy the military stores. Within a quarter of a mile of Lexington Common, hearing the drum beating the minute-men to arms, they hurried on upon the "double quick." Major Pitcairn, finding the Provincials drawn up in line, rode forward, ordering them to disperse; upon their standing firm, his troops fired; two volleys were discharged, the second with fatal effect. The minute-men made scattering return and then dispersed, with a loss of seven killed and nine wounded. The number of the minute-men was about seventy, while that of the British was more than eight hundred. After this encounter, the British marched on towards Concord by Monument St., the Lincoln road, and the old way over Concord Hill, west of the village. (*See Drive No. 16, p. 67.*) On their retreat in the afternoon, they came back by the same route, attacked by the gathering hosts of the patriots at every advantageous point. They were exhausted by their long march, and dispirited by the losses they had sustained. Their first stand in the town was made on a hill a mile and a half west of the Common, where the old and new Concord roads come together. (A granite slab with a suitable inscription stands at the foot of the hill.) Here great efforts were made by the officers to check the retreat and restore order in their broken ranks. But in vain; they were soon driven in much confusion from this position to one on Fiske Hill, still nearer the village. Again the attempt was renewed, but the patriots,

> THIS BLUFF
> WAS USED AS A RALLYING POINT
> BY THE BRITISH
> APRIL 19, 1775.
> AFTER A SHARP FIGHT
> THEY RETREATED TO FISKE HILL
> FROM WHICH THEY WERE DRIVEN
> IN GREAT CONFUSION.

emboldened by their success and sheltered by a breastwork of fence rails, made it impossible to withstand the hot and incessant fire. Here Major Pitcairn was thrown from his horse and the animal was captured with all his accoutrements (See p. 58). From this point the retreat became a confused rout, which was not checked until the flying foe

MUNROE TAVERN.

met Percy's reinforcement half a mile beyond the Common towards Boston. This was in the vicinity of the Munroe Tavern. The British troops had been on the march since ten o'clock of the night before, and, since leaving Concord, had been fighting their way through companies of minute-men gathering along the road. They now had a brief rest under the protection of Percy's fresh troops and two pieces of artillery. For two hours they remained here, pillaging and burning houses, killing cattle and firing in various directions to keep back the patriot host. After dressing their wounded at the Munroe Tavern, eating and drinking whatever they could find, and killing the bar-tender who had served them, they piled up the furniture in one of the rooms, set it on fire, and continued their retreat through the town, hard pressed on every side. Such, in brief, is the story of that day's scenes of outrage and death in Lexington.

MAIN ST., LOOKING NORTH.

MONUMENT. — INSCRIPTION WRITTEN BY REV. JONAS CLARKE.

HISTORICAL TABLETS AND MONUMENTS ALONG THE LINE.

In the year 1884, the town made an appropriation of $1,500 to mark places of historic interest for the information of visitors and to perpetuate a knowledge of important events and sites within our borders. Coming from the direction of Boston, in the village of East Lexington, on Main St., a short distance above the Follen Church, is seen the house, marked by a tablet, of Jonathan Harrington. He was the fifer boy of Capt. Parker's company,

Jonathan Harrington House.

JONATHAN HARRINGTON HOUSE.

a mere lad of sixteen at the time of the battle, but lived to the great age of ninety-six years, the last survivor of that valiant company. It is related that on the morning of the 19th of April, 1775, when the alarm was given, his mother roused him from sleep, calling at the chamber door, "Jonathan, Jonathan, get up, the British are coming and something must be done." Half a mile farther, and a mile south of the Common, we come to the old Munroe Tavern, also marked by a tablet, designating it as the headquarters of Earl Percy on that day. On his visit to Lexington, Nov. 5th, 1789, Washington dined here, the dining-hall being in the southeast room of the second story. Below it is the room where the wounds of the British were dressed, and on the right hand of the front door was the bar-room, in the ceiling of which a bullet hole was made by the discharge of a

The Munroe Tavern.

SANDERSON HOUSE.

British musket. The hole is still to be seen. In this room also the fire was kindled which, happily, was extinguished before much damage had been done.

Near the Tavern, a little below and on the same side, is the old Sanderson house, in which a wounded soldier was left by the British, under the care of Mrs. Sanderson. She lived to the remarkable age of one hundred and four years, and used to tell that the British soldier feared that she meant to poison him, and would not take food or drink until some member of the family had

Sanderson House.

tasted it. Asked in old age, what she gave him, she used to say, "Every now and then I gave him a *diivilich honing.*" In this house was born Lewis Downing, the famous coach builder.

Cannon Tablets. A little farther on towards the village is seen a granite slab, indicating the position of one of Earl Percy's cannon, and recording the fact that several buildings were burned in the vicinity. In the well near by, the Widow Mulliken concealed the family

MERRIAM HOUSE.

silver. Her husband's noted clock-making shop stood here and was destroyed. Thirty rods nearer the village, in the yard of the High School building (*See p. 61*), is a stone cannon marking the spot, then a hill of considerable height, where another British field piece was

ON THE HILL TO THE SOUTH
WAS PLANTED
ONE OF THE BRITISH FIELD PIECES
APRIL 19, 1775,
TO COMMAND THE VILLAGE
AND ITS APPROACHES,
AND NEAR THIS PLACE
SEVERAL BUILDINGS WERE BURNED.

planted to cover the retreat. It is pointed in the direction of the old meeting-house, which stood on the Common. Probably here was fired the shot which passed through the sacred edifice and lodged in the ground beyond. The ball was dug up and given to Harvard College, but has long since disappeared.

Merriam House. A short distance beyond, on the opposite side of the street, stands a venerable house, then occupied by the Merriam family; as stated on the tablet, it was pillaged and set on fire, but unsuccessfully, and the house still remains, being probably 160 years old.

Hayward Tablet. Passing through the village (*See p. 12 for description of the Common.*) and by the British route over Concord Hill, a mile beyond we come to another granite slab standing in the wall in front of a farmhouse. Here, in the yard, young Hayward of Acton, pursuing the foe, stopped to drink at the well, when a British soldier came out of the house, which he had entered for plunder, and raising his gun said, "You are a dead man." "So are you," Hayward replied. Both fired at the same moment; the

> AT THIS WELL
> APRIL 19 1775
> JAMES HAYWARD OF ACTON
> MET A BRITISH SOLDIER
> WHO RAISING HIS GUN SAID
> YOU ARE A DEAD MAN
> AND SO ARE YOU REPLIED HAYWARD
> BOTH FIRED THE SOLDIER
> WAS INSTANTLY KILLED
> AND HAYWARD MORTALLY WOUNDED.

soldier was instantly killed, but Hayward survived until the next day. His powder-horn, through which the British bullet passed, is preserved in his native town. In a corner of the field opposite the house are graves of soldiers, and over the hill towards Concord, near the bluff where the first stand within the borders of Lexington was made, are other graves; no pains were taken to mark the spot and it is now impossible to tell where they are. Graves of British soldiers who fell on the retreat were made in several places, but the exact localities cannot be now identified. Eleven British graves are to be seen in the town of Lincoln (*See Drive No. 14, p. 66*).

OTHER POINTS OF INTEREST.

Parker Homestead In the southwest portion of the town, in the district called "Kite End," and about two miles from the central village, is the Parker homestead (*See Drive No. 9, p. 65*). It has been occupied by the Parker family since 1710, when they came to Lexington from Reading. Here Capt. John Parker was living in 1775, in a house torn down many years since to give place to the present cottage.

PARKER MONUMENT.

From this place he was summoned by the alarm bell on the morning of the 19th of April to assemble his minute-men on the Common; and here he died in the September following. His son, John, succeeded him in the ownership of the farm, and here his grandson, Theodore Parker, was born in 1810, in the old house whose position is marked by a monument placed there by his devoted parishioners. Theodore Parker grew up to manhood, working on the farm through the season, and attending the district school in the winter. He was a studious lad, devoted to books, and reading whatever he could borrow in the neighborhood, or from the village library. In the woods behind the present house, on a hill overlooking the farm, are the ledges where he spent many leisure hours in study. The school was a mile away on the old Concord turnpike, towards Boston, near the present schoolhouse, but on the opposite side of the road. Under the instruction of young collegians, who generally taught the school in winter, he began the study of Latin and Greek, and fitted himself to enter Harvard College without other assistance, giving all his spare time from farm work to the preparatory studies. To the end of his life he cherished a fond remembrance of the scenes of his youth, and he delighted to visit them to refresh his weary body and brain in communion with Nature. On a hill (*See Drive No. 3, p. 64*), between the Parker house and the school is seen a tall pine towering above the surrounding woods, and visible from many points in the town. It stands by the roadside near the Cutler homestead and Parker passed it daily on his way to and from school. He induced the owner to spare it when the rest of the forest was cut down.

A quarter of a mile towards the village, on Spring St. and Concord Avenue, we come to the Phinney place, owned and occupied by Mr. Webster Smith, but for nearly a century the home of the Phinney family.

Elias Phinney, Esq., was clerk of the Middlesex County Court for thirty years, living here and riding daily to and from the sessions at Concord, Cambridge and Lowell. He was an extensive and skillful farmer, and the first imported cattle in Massachusetts were kept on his farm. The improved methods of agriculture, the best labor-saving machinery, the finest stock, the most valuable fruits and vegetables, whatever promised to advance the interests of farming, found in him an earnest advocate. His farm drew many visitors from all parts of the state, and his experiments were the means of instruction and profit to a wide circle. The views from the high lands of the farm upon the western hills and to the Wachusett are among the finest in Lexington. The house erected by Mr. Phinney was destroyed by fire a few years since and has never been re-built.

Cary Farm. Coming towards the village a short distance, an old and little-used road on the left leads by the Cary farm (*See Drive No. 15, p. 67*), the beautiful summer home of Miss Alice B. Cary, the daughter of Maria Hastings Cary, the founder of the

Other Points of Interest. 37

public library (*See p. 58*). Here Mrs. Cary was born and here was the home of her ancestors for many generations. The farm is an extensive and valuable one, and the noble trees around the house, the fine lawn in front, the substantial stone walls, the large gardens and conservatories, the numerous and spacious buildings, give the place an attractive

RESIDENCE OF MISS CARY.

appearance. This farm, containing about two hundred acres with its extensive woodlands, was offered to the State by Mrs. Cary for the agricultural school which was, however, located in a more advantageous position at Amherst. An entrance to the estate from Middle St., on the northeast side, brings it much nearer to the village, but the old road is the only one open to the public. Returning to Spring St., which we left near the Phinney place, and proceeding towards the village, we have, on the left, for a considerable distance, the beautiful Cary woods.

Grapevine Corner. Following Spring St. to Middle St., and continuing on the latter, past Grapevine Corner, we come to "Valleyfield Farm," now owned by Mr. Goldthwaite, one of the most

MULLIKEN OAK.

productive and valuable in the town. It forms one of four tracts of land granted by the proprietors of Cambridge to Matthew Bridge, and embraced, altogether, six hundred acres. Since it passed out of the Bridge family, it has been owned by several different proprietors, each of whom has added improvements, increasing its value and making it more attractive. A large extent of reclaimed swamp-land belongs to this farm, from which heavy crops are obtained. The rambling house, evidently of many additions, and the spacious barn are picturesque.

Waltham Street. Returning to Grapevine Corner and pursuing our way to the village, we pass, on the left, the avenue leading to the house of Dr. R. M. Lawrence. It stands on the southern slope of Loring Hill, high above the street and almost concealed by a heavy growth of forest trees, with which the hill is crowned. From the house and grounds, looking westward, is a fine view, over fields

Other Points of Interest. 39

and woods dotted with farmhouses, into the adjoining town of Lincoln. Nearer the village, on the northern slope of Loring Hill, is the new and elegant house of Hon. A. E. Scott, commanding a prospect of rare beauty across the meadows to Davis and Concord Hills in the north, and to Hancock Heights in the east, with the village lying between.

WALTHAM ST., LOOKING SOUTH-WEST.

Still farther towards the village is the house of Mr. E. A. Mulliken, close beside which stands a giant oak that has numbered perhaps three or four centuries in its growth. It is said to mark the geographical centre of Lexington, a fact ascertained by an actual survey made in the last century, when a new meeting-house was to be built for the town. As we enter the village on Waltham St., the extensive meadows lying on Vine Brook form a pleasing feature of the scene. The broad sweep of fields, backed by wooded hills, where many beautiful dwellings with their gardens, orchards and lawns are seen, form a rare picture of rural peace and beauty. The plain on which the village stands is almost encircled by hills. Only where the North Brook leaves the plain on its way to the Shawsheen, and Vine Brook, on the southeast, seeks the same river, are there breaks in the enclosing hills.

THE MASSACHUSETTS HOUSE AND MUZZEY HOMESTEAD.

Main Street. Adjoining the Town Hall, on Main St., towards Boston, we pass the Massachusetts House, now used as a hotel. This building was erected by the State, in 1876, on the Centennial grounds at Philadelphia, for the state officials; after the close of the exhibition it was purchased and removed here by Mr. David Muzzey. It is now a favorite resort of visitors in the summer and autumn, and of sleighing parties in the winter. Next it, and used as a "Cottage," is the Muzzey homestead. Following Main St., and crossing Vine Brook, we pass, on the right, the site of the Baptist Church, erected about sixty years since for the use of the society, but within recent years greatly enlarged and improved. The edifice was destroyed by fire on the 13th

THE RUSSELL HOUSE.

of May, 1891. Just beyond, at the junction of the Woburn road with Main St., stands the Russell House, a spacious and comfortable hotel which accommodates many guests both in summer and in winter. Nearly opposite are the house and grounds of Mr. Lewis Hunt, occupying a delightful location; and on Bloomfield and Mt. Vernon Sts., just beyond, are many new and pleasant dwellings. Pursuing our way

towards Boston, we pass, on the left, the farm of Mr. James S. Munroe,
a place of great natural beauty. Farther on, we pass, on the
East Lexington. right, the spacious summer residence of Col. William A.
Tower, standing high above the street and overlooking a
wide sweep of country to the east. Entering the village of East Lex-

RESIDENCE OF COL. W. A. TOWER.

ington, at the corner of Maple St., near the house of Mr. Walter Wellington, stands a magnificent elm, sixteen feet in circumference six feet above the ground, one of the largest in the town and at least one hundred and seventy-five years old. The tradition is that it was pulled up by the grandfather of Jonathan Harrington (*See p. 31*) while riding and used as a whip. Reaching home, he planted it without thought or care, but it grew vigorously and has attained gigantic proportions. It still appears sound and vigorous. On the opposite corner is the Pierce homestead, now owned by Mr. Lockwood. The Follen Church, not far below, is a neat, octagonal edifice, with a graceful spire, and having a pleasant and convenient audience-room. It was planned by Dr. Charles Follen, the first pastor of the society, and built under his superintendence. The beautiful communion table and the pulpit with its symbolic carving were also designed by him. The tragic story of his death on the steamer Lexington, while coming from New York to attend the dedication of this edifice, is remembered by the people of the town as one of the most sorrowful events in its history. On the day of dedication the congregation assembled for the service and waited long for their beloved

WELLINGTON ELM.

pastor, whom they were never again to behold in the flesh. Adjoining the church on the south is the house in which he lived and where he preached before the church was built. Ralph Waldo Emerson also preached in this house for a time when pastor of the society. A few rods below, on the left, is the Morrell house, owned by Mrs. Dana, surrounded by beautiful trees and gardens. East Lexington contains many pleasant dwellings and by reason, also, of its beautiful trees and the picturesque hills under which it is built, is an attractive part of the town. The views from Mt. Independence are very fine. Fifty years ago this section of the town was famous for its fur-dressing business carried on by Mr. Eli Robbins and Mr. Ambrose Morrell.

Southerly Lexington. Turning out of Main St., opposite the "Brick Store," into Pleasant St., we follow the road for about a mile to the Wellington homestead, on Concord Avenue, now owned and occupied by Mr. Cornelius Wellington. It has been the home of his

FOLLEN CHURCH.

ancestors for six or seven generations, reaching back a hundred and eighty years, and in it resided Benjamin Wellington, the first prisoner taken by the British. The farm is a productive one, and the substantial house, with fine lawn and beautiful trees in front, the large garden filled with old-fashioned flowers, the extensive views to the north, with the village in the distance, and to the east, over meadows and hills, to Arlington Heights, make it a most attractive place. On Pleasant St.,

Other Points of Interest. 45

MAIN ST., LOOKING NORTH. FOLLEN HOUSE ON THE RIGHT.

just below, is the farm of Mr. Charles A. Wellington, having buildings and grounds hardly less delightful. Proceeding up the Concord turnpike (West), we soon reach Blossom St. on the right, a road rightly named, winding in and out among farmhouses and orchards with pleasant views opening at almost every point. This portion of the

WELLINGTON HOMESTEAD.

town was formerly known as "Smith End," nearly every farm belonging to some member of that prolific family. At the large old farmhouse of Mr. Abram Smith, on this street, is another of those huge elms for which Lexington is noted, with a trunk not less than sixteen feet in circumference, and a top of great height and area; it has witnessed probably the birth and death of six generations. Continuing through the sinuosities of either Allen or Blossom Sts., we come out upon Waltham St., and return to the village.

Hancock Street. Starting from the Common and proceeding up Hancock St., we pass, on the right, the fine places of Mr. M. H. Merriam and Mr. B. F. Brown, having extensive grounds

RESIDENCE OF MR. M. H. MERRIAM.

adorned with a variety of noble trees. Both dwellings occupy elevated sites and have a charming outlook over the village. Farther up the street, and on the opposite side, adjoining the old Hancock-Clarke house, is the estate of Mrs. Mary Brigham. Here is seen a magnificent elm having a double trunk and a symmetrical top that sweeps the ground in a circle five or six rods in diameter (*See p. 24*). It is known

Lexington.

HANCOCK ST., LOOKING SOUTH.

to be above one hundred and twenty years old, and is, apparently, in the vigor of youth. Undoubtedly it is one of the most graceful and beautiful trees in New England. In the rear of the house, on a long ridge, is a noble grove of oak and walnut trees that extends across several adjoining estates, and adds much to the beauty of the vicinity.

RESIDENCE OF MR. B. F. BROWN.

On the opposite side of the street is the entrance to the large estate of Mr. Francis B. Hayes, embracing four hundred acres of gardens, lawns, fields, orchards and meadows, with extensive forests of pine and oak crowning the highlands. These grounds are not usually open to the public.

Continuing up Hancock St., we pass the home of Mr. George O. Whiting, at the corner of Adams St., occupying a fine, elevated site with large grounds, and having an extensive view of hills and mountains in the northwestern horizon.

The next house beyond is noted as the home of Dr. Joseph Fiske, a surgeon in the army of the Revolution. He was living here at the time of the battle, and dressed the wounded after the encounter on the Common and during the day. He belonged to a family of physicians, three

RESIDENCE OF MR. G. O. WHITING.

generations of whom resided in Lexington. Passing Revere St. on the left, we come to the pleasant home and farm of Mr. Francis E. Ballard, a place neatly kept, well-tilled and productive. A lane on the left leads to the site of the old Tidd house, recently pulled down after standing for two hundred years. A noble elm, probably of equal age, close to the North Brook, marks the spot where lived and died five or

Other Points of Interest. 51

six generations of a family once prominent in the town, but having no representative here at the present time.

North Lexington. Passing up Hancock St., by the schoolhouse, we have, on the height of ground, another fine view of the hills and mountains in the distant horizon. Pursuing our way on Bedford St., we pass some of the largest and best farms in Lexington, notably those of Mr. Wetherbee, Mr. John P. Reed, and, on a back road, that of Mr. Stimpson, formerly the Hammon Reed place. This portion of the town was taken up at an early day by William Reed, and

FISKE HOUSE.

the neighborhood was largely owned by his descendants for many generations. Across the brook at the foot of the hill towards Bedford, is seen an old house among the trees, which is known as the Lawrence homestead. Here the Lawrence family located in the early settlement of the town, and from this place removed to Groton, where those princely merchants, Abbott and Amos Lawrence, were born. Returning towards the village, past the North Lexington station, in a beautiful grove is the substantial house of Mr. Kramer, formerly known as the Cushing place, and just beyond, on the right, lies the extensive and valuable farm of Mr. F. O. Vaille. The house and barns are on a gentle elevation a little way from the street, and from them is a fine outlook on every side over broad meadows, pastures and fields. Before reaching the village we pass, on the left, the pleasant homestead of Prof. H. E. Holt.

LAWRENCE HOUSE.

Merriam's Hill. Merriam St., leading out of Main St. adjoining the Merriam homestead (*See p. 7*), crosses the railroad track and terminates at the crown of the hill, in plain view of the Hayes mansion. On the left are the large house and grounds of Mr. Charles C. Goodwin, occupying a commanding position, and overlooking the village, while, opposite, is the new house of Robert P. Clapp, Esq., from which the long range of the New Hampshire hills forms a

Other Points of Interest.

pleasing picture. At the corner of Oakland and Merriam Sts. stands the quaint and pretty Episcopal Church, having a pleasant audience-room with an elaborate altar and reading-desk. Passing up Oakland St. until we reach the summit of the hill, we find here a number of new houses of modern architecture, having about them an air of comfort

RESIDENCE OF MR. C. C. GOODWIN.

and refinement. The location is especially attractive for the fine views which it affords of Arlington Heights, East Lexington and the Waltham hills. No spot in the vicinity of the village is better worth visiting than this cluster of pleasant houses on Oakland St. and the summit of the hill in the rear.

Lexington.

Concord Hill. Monument St. leads from the Common, past the Roman Catholic Church and over Concord Hill. At its junction with Lincoln St. is a triangular piece of ground containing about three acres, which has recently been purchased for a park. It is given to the Field and Garden Club (*See p. 62*), on condition that it be put in order and kept open to public use. The purpose is to spend at least $1,000 in improving it. It is to be known as

MONUMENT ST., LOOKING NORTH.

Hastings Park. An avenue on the right leads to the home of Mr. George W. Robinson. It stands upon the southern slope of Concord Hill, surrounded by a variety of trees, amid extensive grounds.

The North Brook takes its rise on the grounds in front of Mr. Robinson's house and flows for a long distance through adjoining farms, in nearly a straight line. It deserves our notice from the fact that it once formed the northern boundary of Cambridge. It was called "the eight-mile line." When the Cambridge settlers complained that their lands were too limited, the General Court granted them all the land extending to a line drawn eight miles northwest of their meeting-house, and lying between Woburn on one side and Watertown on the other. Here was the extent of their grant.

Farther up the hill and nearer Monument St. are the places of Messrs. Charles and Walter Mowry, the latter a new and comfortable house, and the former a substantial mansion built many years ago by Mr. Daniel Chandler. On the Lincoln road, south of the new park, the home of Mr. Newell occupies a conspicuous site, and, just beyond, are the wells and pumping station of the Lexington Water Works. From deep springs opened here a supply of pure water is drawn for the use of the town. A scientific analysis proves it to be of the best quality, and there appears to be a moderate supply for the present wants of the town.

56 *Lexington.*

ELM AVENUE, LOOKING EAST.

PUBLIC BUILDINGS.

Hancock School-house.
On Clarke St., at the corner of Forest, stands the substantial and beautiful Hancock Schoolhouse, recently erected by the town at a cost, including the lot, of $60,000 (*See p. 10*). It contains eight school-rooms, besides a hall in the third story, and a sewing and cooking-room. It is designed to hold all the primary and grammar schools of the town, excepting those of East Lexington. The arrangements for warming and ventilating are by the most approved methods, and the rooms are so arranged that the pupils

TOWN HALL, MEMORIAL HALL AND CARY LIBRARY.

may enjoy the full benefit of the sunlight. It is planned to accommodate four hundred pupils, and is supplied with every comfort and convenience for their health and happiness. Probably no school building in the state is better fitted for educational purposes, or presents a finer architectural appearance.

Town Hall.
The Town Hall, on Main St., erected twenty years ago on the site of Bigelow's Hotel and Dr. Dio Lewis' famous school, is a massive structure and is well adapted to the various uses

for which it was designed. The main hall is in the second story and, with the gallery, seats comfortably six or seven hundred persons. It contains a striking picture of the Battle of Lexington, painted by Sandham, which belongs to the Lexington Historical Society, and was purchased, by subscription, at a cost of $4000. There is also in the hall a beautiful painting of flowers, the gift of the Whitmore family of Boston to the Cary Library. In the third story of the building are two smaller halls, fitted for society and social uses.

Cary Library. On the first floor of the Town Hall building is a spacious room devoted to the Cary Library. The library, founded by the late Maria Hasting Cary of Brooklyn, N. Y., a native of Lexington (*See p. 36*), contains about 13,000 carefully selected volumes, and is open to the free use of the people. It is supported by the income of invested funds and by an annual appropriation of the town for its care and increase. From five to seven hundred new books are added yearly, and the annual circulation amounts to 25,000 volumes. The library is supplied with the leading magazines of the country and with newspapers. Besides many portraits and busts of noted characters, it possesses a large number of valuable and curious relics, illustrating the history of the town. Among these are the identical pistols worn by Major Pitcairn on the 19th of April, 1775, one of which he fired when the command was given to fire on the minutemen. They were captured in the afternoon of that day, with the horse that he rode, during the confusion of the British retreat (*See p. 28*). After-

JOHN HANCOCK.

wards they were presented to Gen. Putnam, by whom they were worn through the war of the Revolution, and a few years since they were given to the town by his great-grandniece. The four pictures of the scenes of the 19th of April, 1775, the drawings for which were made a few weeks after the battle by Amos Doolittle of New Haven, are curious and interesting. A photograph of the original account of the battle on Lexington Common sent by express to Philadelphia on the morning of the 19th, from Watertown, is framed and hung here. The original is preserved in Independence Hall. A large number of relics relating to ancient customs have been gathered, together with much valuable information regarding the early history of the town. The library is open to visitors on every afternoon of the week excepting Sunday, and on alternate evenings (*See p. 72*).

SAMUEL ADAMS.

Memorial Hall. A hall dedicated to the memory of the departed heroes who died for their country, although originally separate, has been opened into the library room. On its walls are handsome marble tablets, inscribed with the names and deeds of the sons of Lexington who have fallen in battle, and, in four niches, are marble statues of Hancock, of Adams, of a minute-man of 1775, and of a soldier of 1861.

Savings Bank. The Town Hall building contains also the Lexington Savings Bank, an institution that has been very carefully and wisely managed, and has deposits amounting to nearly $240,000. For many years it has paid semi-annual dividends of 2½

1775.

1861.

per cent, besides adding to its reserve fund. Deposits are received from residents of the town only.

High School-house. On Main St., just below Woburn, stands the High School building. It was used, until the erection of the present brick building, as the Town Hall (*See p. 33*).

Village Hall. In East Lexington, at the corner of Locust Avenue, stands the "Village Hall." It was originally occupied as a church by the Universalist society, which united with the Follen Church, and, afterwards, by the Roman Catholics, until the erection of their church on Monument St. It is now owned by the town and contains a pleasant little hall as well as the Adams Engine and the Hovey Hook-and-Ladder Houses. The Hancock Engine-house is located on Merriam St.

Adams School-House. Opposite the Follen Church stands the Adams Schoolhouse, which accommodates the primary and grammar schools of East Lexington. It was erected many years ago, and is the third school-building that has stood on this lot. In one of its rooms is the East Lexington branch of the Cary Library.

Manufactures. Lexington has but little manufacturing business, its people being engaged chiefly in agriculture, or in business in neighboring cities. Two establishments, however, are

HIGH SCHOOL BUILDING AND CANNON MONUMENT.

worthy of notice, that of Mr. Matthew H. Merriam, on Oakland St., devoted to the manufacture of leather findings, and employing between thirty and forty persons, chiefly women, and that of Mr. Chas. Grant, on Fletcher St., devoted to the manufacture of all kinds of iron gearing. Each has established a prosperous business.

Churches, Societies, etc. At the present time Lexington contains six churches, five Protestant and one Roman Catholic. It has nine primary and grammar schools, and one high school, containing altogether upwards of four hundred pupils, and having fourteen teachers, including a teacher of music and one of sewing. The town makes an annual appropriation for public schools of about $12,000.

It has five grocery, two drug and two provision stores, besides a number of others, four hotels, a grain mill, a lumber yard, gas works, two post-offices, and five railroad stations. It has a Field and Garden Club devoted to the improvement of the streets and public grounds,

ADAMS SCHOOL HOUSE.

and an Historical Society having a membership of two hundred and forty persons. It has a male chorus of thirty singers which has been under able training for many years, a base-ball and a shooting club, a large number of literary, book, and social clubs, as well as financial associations and secret societies ; in addition to these an efficient Grand Army Post and Women's Relief Corps. The population is slowly but steadily increasing. During the last ten years, there have been many

Public Buildings. 63

new houses erected and a larger gain in population and wealth than in any decade since the settlement of the town. The people are generally in circumstances of prosperity and comfort. For the most part, their houses and grounds present a tidy and tasteful appearance. Beautiful walks and drives abound in the town and its vicinity, and visitors

MAIN STREET, LOOKING SOUTH.

find much to interest them and make their stay pleasant and profitable. It is a town which offers many advantages as a place of residence in its pure and invigorating air, its delightful scenery, its historic associations, and its freedom from annoyances incident to many suburban communities.

DRIVES.

FOLLOWING are a few of the shorter drives around Lexington. They may be combined and varied to an indefinite extent. Many delightful excursions of twenty miles or more may be made, but for these it is impossible to give exact directions. For them, as well as for the shorter drives, it is important to have a good road-map. The most accurate is that published by the Appalachian Mt. Club, taken from the State Topographical Survey, but it gives neither the town boundaries nor the names of roads. For this reason other, less accurate, maps are, perhaps, more useful.

1. **Shawsheen Drive.** Monument St., over Concord Hill, to 2d r. h. road (Wood St.). Follow Wood St., bearing always to the right (*Tophet Swamp, E.*), to Bedford St. Follow Bedford St. (S.) (*past old Lawrence House*) to Lex.— 6 ms., or, taking on Wood St. the 2d l. h. road, follow it to Bedford, and return via Bedford St.— 9 ms.

2. **Short Historic Drive.** Monument St., over Concord Hill, 1½ ms. to "Bluff." (*See tablet there and one at Hayward House, 1 mile from Lex.*) Turning sharply to the left at the "Bluff," follow the new Concord road (Marrett St.) (S. E.) one mile to 3d l. h. road (Middle St). Follow Middle St. (E.) 2 ms. to East Lex. Return via Main St., past historic points, to Lex.— 6 ms.

3. **Mt. Tabor Drive.** Lincoln St. to 4th l. h. road (Weston St.). Follow Weston St., under Mt. Tabor (*in crossing the Concord Turnpike, go N. W. a few rods to the new road instead of following the road between the great boulders*) to the 1st l. h. road beyond Mt. Tabor (North St. or Trapelo Road). Follow North St. (S. E.) to 3d l. h. road (Walnut St.). Follow Walnut St., Concord Turnpike (W.) and Waltham St. to Lex.— 8 ms.

4. **Waverly Oaks Drive.** Waltham St., 2½ ms. to 6th l. h. road (Trapelo Road). Follow Trapelo Road (S. E.) 2 ms. to 4th l. h. road (Mill St.). (*Waverly Oaks, Cascade, and Convalescents' Home at this point.*) Follow Mill St. (N.) one mile to Concord Turnpike. Thence by Concord Turnpike (a few rods) and Winter St. (*past Belmont Spring, worth visiting*) to E. Lex., and by Main St. to Lex.— 9 ms.

5. **Belmont Drive.** Main St. to Pleasant St., E. Lex. Follow Pleasant

Drives. 65

St. to 2d l. h. road (Concord Turnpike). Follow Concord Turnpike (E.), through the "Willows," (*beautiful stretch of road*) to 1st r. h. road (Mill St.). Here take the straight road, over the hill (*fine view*), or follow Mill St., bearing always to the left. Both roads lead to Belmont. Thence follow Pleasant St. (*past Spy Pond*) to Arlington, and return, via Arlington Ave. and Main St. (*note historic tablets*) to Lex. — 10 ms.

6. **Winchester Drive.** Main St. (S. E.), past "Foot of the Rocks" (Arlington Heights) to Forest St. Follow Forest St., over Turkey Hill, to 1st r. h. road (Oak St). Follow Oak St., bearing to the right, to Mystic St. (*Shore of Mystic Lake.*) Follow Mystic St. (N.) to 3d r. h. road (Church St.), which follow to Winchester. Returning on Church St., take Wildwood St. (*on the right*) to Cambridge St. Follow Cambridge St. (N.) to 1st l. h. road (Parker St.) (*a narrow lane through the woods*). Follow Parker St. to Lexington St. and return (W.) 2 ms. to Lex.— 10 ms.; or, on Cambridge St., after leaving Wildwood, take 1st r. h. road (Pond St.) and follow it (*around Horn Pond*) to Woburn. Return by direct road to Lex.—13 ms.

7. **Zion's Hill Drive.** Same route as No. 6 to Oak St. There take l. h. road (Ridge St.) and follow it (*fine views*) down a rather rough, steep hill, to Lexington St. Return (W.) to Lex.— 8 ms.; or, on Ridge St., take 1st r. h. road (High St.) and follow it, down steep hill, to Winchester. Return as in No. 6 — 9 ms.; or, on High St., take 1st r. h. road (Arlington St.) and follow it to Mystic St. (*Shore of Mystic Lake.*) Follow Mystic St. (S.) to Arlington, and return as in No. 5 — 11 ms.

8. **Waltham Drive (1).** Waltham St. to 2d l. h. road (Allen St). By Allen and Blossom Sts. to Concord Turnpike. Follow this (E.) a short distance to 1st r. h. road (Walnut St). Follow Walnut St. one mile (*past Commonwealth Spring*) to 2d r. h. road (Forest St.). By Forest and Lyman Sts. (*past the Lyman Estate*) 2 ms. to Waltham. Return by the straight road (Lexington St.) to Lex.— 10 ms.

9. **Brook St. Drive.** Waltham St. to 1st r. h. road (Middle St., *Grapevine Corner*). Follow Middle St. to 1st l. h. road (Spring St). Follow Spring St. (*past Parker Homestead*) nearly 2 ms. to 4th r. h. road (Lincoln St.), thence (N. W.) a few rods to Brook St. Follow Brook St. one mile to 1st r. h. road (Winter St.). Follow Winter St. (N.

W.) 2 ms. to Lincoln Centre. Returning take, after leaving the Public Library, the 1st left (Lincoln St.) to Lex.— 11 ms.

10. **Durenville Drive.** Woburn St. one mile to Lowell Turnpike. Follow Lowell Turnpike (N.) to 1st r. h. road (Russell St.). Follow Russell St., through Durenville, to 1st l. h. road (Cambridge St.). Follow Cambridge St. (N.) 3 ms. to Burlington. In Burlington, take l. h. road at Congregational Church, and return (1st right, 2d left, 4th right) to Lex.— 11 ms.

11. **Vine Brook Drive.** Hancock St. to 2d r. h. road (Burlington St). Follow Burlington St. 1¼ ms. to 2d l. h. road (Lowell Turnpike). Follow Lowell Turnpike (N. W.) 2 ms. to 1st l. h. road after crossing a brook (Vine Brook). Follow this road (S. W.), taking 1st left, 1st right, 2d left, 1st right, to Bedford. Return via Bedford St. to Lex.— 11 ms.

12. **Arlington Heights Drive.** Main St. to E. Lex. There take Pleasant St. to the 1st l. h. road (Watertown St.). Follow Watertown St. ½ m. to 1st l. h. road (Valley St.). Follow Valley St. to the top of Arlington Heights (*fine view*). Thence follow Park Ave. and Clifton St. (S.) to Belmont. Follow Pleasant St. and Arlington Ave. to "Foot of the Rocks." There take r. h. road (Lowell Turnpike) and follow it to 2d l. h. road (Maple St). Follow Maple St. (*past Peirce's Bridge Station*) to Main St., which follow to Lex.— 11 ms. (*Arlington Heights may be reached directly via Main St. and Park Ave.*)

13. **Cummingsville Drive.** Hancock St. to Adams St. Follow Adams St. to 2d r. h. road (North St.). Follow North St. (*crossing Lowell Turnpike*) 1½ ms. to 1st r. h. road. (*It is a small wood road leading off opposite a wide intervale.*) Follow this wood road, through the farm of the Hon. John Cummings, to Burlington St. Follow Burlington St. (E.) through Cummingsville, to Woburn. Return by direct road to Lex.— 11 ms.; or, at Burlington St., take l. h. and, taking 1st left, 1st right, and 1st left, return by Reed's mill to Lowell Turnpike. Follow Lowell Turnpike and Adams St. to Lex.— 9 ms.

14. **Lincoln Drive.** Lincoln St. direct to Lincoln. At the Public Library keep straight ahead (Concord Road) one mile to Sandy Pond. Follow the road around the farther side of the pond, 2 ms., to the Concord

Turnpike. Follow Concord Turnpike (S. E.) to 1st r. h. road. Follow this road, over the high hill (*fine view from the reservoir, a short walk to the left*), to Lincoln. Return via North and Weston Sts. to Lex.— 12 ms.

15. **Waltham Drive (2)**. Lincoln St. to 4th l. h. road (Weston St.). A few rods on Weston St., turn abruptly to the left, into a wooded, unfrequented road (Shade St.), which follow (*past the Cary Estate*) to 1st l. h. road (Spring St.). Follow Spring St. (*past the Parker Homestead*) 4 ms. to Waltham. Return via Lexington St. to Lex.— 11 ms.

16. **Concord Drive**. Monument St. direct to Concord (*route of the British*). See objects of interest there (*Bartlett's Guide*). Returning, take, at Emerson's house, the r. h. road (Concord Turnpike). Follow this 5 ms. to 5th l. h. road (Weston St). Return by Weston St. (N. E.) and Lincoln St. to Lex.— 14 ms.

17. **Hancock and Adams Drive**. Hancock and Adams Sts. to Lowell Turnpike. Follow Turnpike (N.) a few rods to r. h. (Burlington) road. Follow this (*past Reed's mill*) to Burlington. (*At 1½ ms. on Burlington road notice Reed estate on right and, on left, the old Sewall House, first stopping place of Hancock and Adams.*) In Burlington, take l. h. (Bedford) road (W.) at the Congregational Church, and follow it, bearing always to the right, 2 ms., to an old house standing on a knoll on the left. Near this house, in the woods, is the cellar of the Wyman house, final refuge of Hancock and Adams. Continuing to Billerica road, turn sharply to the right, and return via Burlington — 14 ms.

18. **Waltham Drive (3)**. Monument St., towards Concord, to 1st l. h. road (½ mile) beyond "Bluff" (*see No. 2*). Follow this road through the woods to its junction with Lincoln St. Follow Lincoln St. a few rods (S. W.) to its junction with the Concord Turnpike. Follow Concord Turnpike (W.) a short distance, to 1st l. h. road, which follow (*straight ahead*) and then by Winter and West Sts., 4 ms., to Kendall Green. Return via Waltham to Lex.— 14 ms.

19. **Walden Pond Drive**. Lincoln St. to Lincoln. At the Public Library take road to railroad station. A short distance beyond the railroad crossing take 1st r. h. road to Walden St., leading to Walden Pond. Returning on Walden St., take 1st l. h. road which leads (*near Sandy Pond*) to Lincoln. Return via North and Weston Sts. to Lex.— 14

ms.; or, at Walden Pond, continue on to Concord, and return thence by direct road — 16 ms.

20. **Old Bedford Road Drive** Hancock St to 2d r. h road (Burlington St.). Follow Burlington St to 1st l h road (Grove St.). Follow Grove St. through the woods (*bearing always to the left*) to Bedford St. Return via Bedford St (S.) to Lex.— 8 ms.; or, at Bedford St. turn to the right to Bedford. There take Spring St. to Bedford Springs (*Hotel*). Continue thence to Billerica road, which follow (S.) back to Bedford St — 14 ms

21. **Nutting's Pond Drive.** Bedford and Spring Sts. to Bedford Springs. Continuing thence, take 2d right and 1st left, 2 ms., to Nutting's Pond. Crossing the pond take 1st l. h. road, and return through So. Billerica and Bedford to Lex.— 16 ms.

22. **Medford Drive.** Main St. to Arlington. Thence, via Charlestown and Curtis Sts. to top of College Hill. (*Tufts' College; fine view; old Powder House in vicinity.*) From top of College Hill follow College, Royall (*Royall House*), and Main Sts. to Medford (*quaint and interesting town*). At Medford Centre follow Riverside Ave. to the Cradock House (*oldest house in New England*). Return via Medford, West Medford, and Arlington — 13 ms.

23. **Mt. Auburn Drive.** Main St. to Park Ave. (Arlington Heights). Follow Park Ave. to Summit and proceed thence, via Eastern Ave. and Spring Pl., straight down to Pleasant St. Follow Pleasant St. (S. W.) a short distance to Brighton St. Follow Brighton St. (*crossing Fitchburg R. R.*) to Concord Turnpike. Follow this (E.) a short distance to Fresh Pond Drive, which take, half way around the pond, to an exit upon Cushing St., which follow (S. E.) to Mt. Auburn. Returning, follow Belmont St. (*past Payson Park and other fine estates*) to North St. Follow North St. (*through Gipsy Woods*) to Waverly. Return, via Mill St., Concord Turnpike, Watertown St., to Lex.— 15 ms.

24. **Virginia Drive.** Monument St. to Wood St. (*see No. 1.*) Follow Wood St. to 1st !. h. road and follow this to the Virginia Road (1st right). Follow Virginia Road (*bearing always to the left*) to its junction with the Concord road (*Merriam's corner, of historic interest*). Return via direct road to Lex.— 14 ms.

Drives.

25. Weston and Norumbega Drive. Lincoln St. to Weston St. (*see* No. 3). Thence, under Mt. Tabor, past High Rock, and through a beautiful wooded road, 5 ms. to Weston. Thence, following the direct road to Waltham, take the 2d r. h. road to Roberts' Mills (*see Norumbega Tower*). Return via Waltham to Lex.— 16 ms. ; or, Norumbega may be reached direct, through Waltham, returning the same way — 12 ms.

Following, are suggestions for a few of the

LONGER DRIVES.

26. Wellesley Drive. To Wellesley, via Waltham and Auburndale (*good, though expensive, hotel at Wellesley*). See Wellesley College, Hunnewell Estate, and Baker Estate, and return same way — 28 ms.

27. Wayside Inn Drive. To Wayside Inn (So. Sudbury) via Weston and Wayland (*good hotel at Wayland*). Return through Sudbury Centre (*Wadsworth Monument*) — 28 ms.

28. Middlesex Fells Drive. To Middlesex Fells, via Arlington and Medford, and around Spot Pond, (*Hotel Langwood at Wyoming*). Return via Stoneham and Winchester, past Reservoir and through Highland Ave. (*fine views*) — 25 ms.

29. Magog Drive. To Acton (*of historic interest*), via Concord (*past the Reformatory*) and thence to Magog Lake (*country tavern*). Return via Carlisle and Bedford — 30 ms.

30. Robbins' Hill Drive. To Robbins' Hill, Chelmsford (*fine view ; good hotel at Chelmsford*) via Bedford. Return via Billerica — 30 ms.

31. So. Natick Drive. To So. Natick (*Eliot monument ; good hotel*) via Newton Lower Falls. Return via Weston — 30 ms.

32. Concord River Drive. To Fairhaven Bay (*Sudbury River*) via Lincoln. Return through Nine-acre Corner (*see White Pond*) and Concord. Crossing the river, continue along its west bank, over Punkatasset Hill, bearing always to the right, through Bedford to Lex.— 24 ms.

In addition to these, pleasant excursions are to Waltham, taking boats there to Riverside, on the Charles River; or, to Concord, taking boats there and rowing down stream, or up the Assabet or Sudbury Rivers. *For a short trip it is best to follow the Assabet (North branch).*

WALKS.

There are many beautiful walks over the hills and through the unfrequented roads of Lexington, but, as they lead, in general, over private property, it is impossible to outline them.

MAIN ST., LOOKING NORTH-WEST, EAST LEXINGTON.

CHURCHES.

FIRST CONGREGATIONAL (UNITARIAN) SOCIETY, *Elm Ave.*, REV. C. A. STAPLES, *Pastor.* — Sunday Services, 10.30 A.M., and (usually) 7 P.M. Sunday-school, 12 M. Young People's Guild, alternate Sundays, 7 P.M. Unitarian Club, 1st Monday of each month (except through the summer) 7.30 P.M. Ladies' Benevolent Society and Lend-a-Hand Society have frequent meetings.

HANCOCK CONGREGATIONAL (ORTHODOX) SOCIETY, *Bedford and Hancock Streets*, REV. IRVING MEREDITH, *Pastor.* — Sunday Services, 10.30 A.M. and 7 P.M. Communion Service, 1st Sunday in January, March, May, July, September, and November, at 3 P.M. Sabbath School, 12 M. Y. P. S. of Christian Endeavor, Mondays, 7.30 P.M. Ladies' Meeting, Wednesdays, 3 P.M. Prayer Meeting, Fridays, 7.45 P.M.

BAPTIST SOCIETY, Services held, at present, in Town Hall, REV. L. B. HATCH, *Pastor.* — Sunday Services, 10.30 A.M., and 7 P.M. Sabbath School, 12 M. Prayer Meeting, Thursdays, at 7.45 P.M. Y. P. S. of Christian Endeavor, Tuesdays, 7.45 P.M.

FOLLEN CHURCH (UNITARIAN CONGREGATIONAL), *Main St.*, East Lexington, ———, *Pastor.* — Sunday Services, 10.45 A.M. Sunday-school, 12 M. Ladies' Sewing Society, alternate Thursday afternoons.

CHURCH OF OUR REDEEMER (EPISCOPALIAN) *Merriam Street*, REV. ALFRED B. NICHOLS, *Minister in Charge.* — Sunday Services, Morning Prayer, 10.45 A.M.; Evening Prayer (June to October) 7.30 P.M. Communion, 1st and 3d Sundays of the month. Woman's Guild, 1st Thursday in the month (October to May).

ST. BRIDGET'S CHURCH (ROMAN CATHOLIC), *Monument St.*, REV. P. J. KAVANAUGH, *Pastor.*

LEXINGTON POST-OFFICE.

L. G. BABCOCK, *Postmaster*.

OFFICE HOURS. — 7 A.M. to 8 P.M. Sundays, 1.30 to 2.30 P.M.
MAILS CLOSE — 8.30 A. M., 12.45 and 5.50 P.M. Sundays, 4.30 P.M.
MAILS READY FOR DELIVERY — 7.45 A.M., 1.20 and 5.30 P.M. Sundays, 2 P.M.

EAST LEXINGTON POST OFFICE.

AUGUSTUS CHILDS, *Postmaster*.

MAILS CLOSE — 8.30 A.M. and 4.30 P.M.
MAILS READY FOR DELIVERY — 7.45 A.M., and 5.10 P.M.

CARY LIBRARY.

MISS WHITCHER, *Librarian*.

HOURS. — Monday, Wednesday, and Friday, 3 to 6 P.M. Tuesday, Thursday and Saturday, 2 to 9 P.M.

EAST LEXINGTON BRANCH.

MISS HOLBROOK, *Librarian*.

HOURS. — Monday, Tuesday, Wednesday and Friday, 12.15 to 1.30 P.M., and 5 to 8 P.M. Saturday, 4 to 8 P.M.

INDEX.

Academy, Lexington, 21.
Acton, 34, 69.
Adams, Samuel, 25, 27, 59, 67.
Adams St., 49, 66.
Adams Engine House, 60.
Adams School house, 60, 62.
Allen St., 47, 65.
Area, 5.
Arlington, 65, 68, 69.
Arlington Heights, 44, 53, 66, 68.
Assabet River, 70.
Auburndale, 69.
Augustus, John, 16, 20.

Baptist Society, 41, 71.
Base-ball Club, 62.
Bedford, 64, 66, 68, 69.
Bedford Springs, 68.
Bedford St., 7, 12, 51, 64, 66, 68.
Belfry, 7, 8, 18.
Belfry Hill, 18, 26.
Belmont, 64, 66.
Belmont Springs, 64.
Bigelow's Hotel, 57.
Billerica, 25, 69.
Bloomfield St., 41.
Blossom St., 46, 65.
"Bluff," 27, 64, 67.
Boulder, 14.
Bowes, Lucy, 24.
Bridge Grant, 38.
Brook St., 65.
Buckman Tavern, 6, 7, 14.
Burlington, 25, 66, 67.
Burlington St., 66.
Burying Ground, 19.

Cambridge, 6, 7, 54.
Cambridge Farms, 6.
Cannon Tablets, 33, 61.
Carlisle, 69.
Cary Farm, 36, 67.
Cary Library, 18, 36, 57, 58, 61, 72.
Cemetery, Old, 19.
Charles River, 5, 70.
Chelmsford, 69.

Childs Monument, 20, 22.
Churches, 7, 13, 19, 21, 41, 43, 53, 54, 61, 71.
Clarke, Rev. Jonas, 20, 24, 30.
Clarke House, 22, 47.
Clarke Tomb, 20.
Clarke St., 18, 57.
Clubs, 54, 62, 71.
College Hill, 68.
Common, The 7, 12, 27.
Commonwealth Spring, 65.
Concord, 27, 28, 67, 68, 69.
Concord Hill, 27, 34, 39, 54, 64.
Concord River, 5, 69, 70.
Concord Turnpike, 35, 46, 64, 66, 67, 68.
Cradock House, 68.
Cummingsville, 66.

Davis Hill, 19, 39.
Doolittle, Amos, 59.
Downing, Lewis, 33.
Drives, 5, 63, 64.
Durenville, 66.

East Lexington, 31, 42, 53, 60, 64, 70.
"Eight-mile line," 54.
Elm Ave., 12, 15, 21, 56.
Elms, Notable, 13, 24, 42, 46, 47.
Emerson, R. W., 43, 67
Estabrook, Benj., 7, 20.
Estabrook, Joseph, 8, 20.
Eustis, William, 20.
Everett, Edward, 17.

Fairhaven Bay, 69.
Field and Garden Club, 54, 62.
Fares, Railroad, 5.
Fire Department, 60.
Fiske, David, 16, 50.
Fiske, Joseph, 50.
Fiske Hill, 27.
Fletcher St., 61.
Follen, Charles, 43.
Follen Church, 31, 43, 44, 60, 71.
Follen House, 43, 45.
"Foot of the Rocks," 65, 66.
Forest St., 18, 57.
Fresh Pond, 68.

Grand Army Post, 62.
Grant Elm, 13.
Grapevine Corner, 38, 65.
Grove St., 68.

Hancock, Ebenezer, 23.
Hancock, Rev. John, 7, 20, 22.
Hancock, Gov. John, 7, 22, 24, 27, 58, 67.
Hancock, Thomas, 22, 23.
Hancock Church, 21, 71.
Hancock-Clarke Elm, 24, 47.
Hancock-Clarke House, 22, 23, 47.
Hancock-Clarke Tomb, 20, 21.
Hancock Engine House, 60.
Hancock Heights, 39.
Hancock Mansion, 23.
Hancock Schoolhouse, 10, 57.
Hancock St., 21, 22, 47, 66, 67, 68.
Harrington, Caleb, 18.
Harrington House, 15.
Harrington, Jonathan, 31, 42.
Hastings Park, 54.
Hayes Estate, 49, 52.
Hayward, James, 34, 64.
Herlarkenden, Robt., 7.
High Rock, 69.
High School Building, 33, 60, 61.
Historical Society, 18, 58, 62.
History, 6.
Horn Pond, 65.
Hotels, 40, 41, 62.
Hovey Hook and Ladder House, 60.

Incorporation, 6.
Inscriptions, 13, 16, 27, 30, 33, 59, 61, 64, 65.

Kendall Green, 67.
" Kite End," 35.
Kossuth, 17.

Lafayette, 17.
Lawrence House, 51, 64.
Lewis, Dio, 57.
Lincoln, 34, 66, 69.
Lincoln St., 54, 64, 65, 66, 67, 69.
Line of Battle, 14.
Locust Ave., 60.
Lord Lexington, 6.
Loring Hill, 38.
Lowell Turnpike, 66, 67.

Magog Lake, 69.
Main St., 13, 27, 29, 40, 45, 60, 63, 64, 68, 70.
Male Chorus, 62.
Manufactures, 61.
Map of the Town, 4.
Map, Sketch, 1775, 26.
Maps, 64.
Maple St., 42, 66.
Marrett St., 64.
Massachusetts House, 40.
Medford, 68, 69.
Meeting Houses, 7, 9, 13, 34.
Meeting-House Monument, 7, 13.
Memorial Hall, 57, 59.
Merriam House, 7, 14.
Merriam, Benj., 34.
Merriam's Corner, 68.
Merriam's Hill, 52.
Merriam St., 52, 60.
Middle St., 37, 64, 65.
Middlesex Fells, 69.
Military Affairs, 9.
Minute-Men, 9, 14, 17, 27, 31, 58.
Monadnock Mt., 5.
Monument, The, 8, 16, 30.
Monument St., 7, 12, 18, 27, 54, 64, 67.
Morrell, Ambrose 43.
Mt. Auburn, 68.
Mt. Independence, 44.
Mt. Tabor, 64, 69.
Mt. Vernon St., 41.
Mulliken House, 33.
Mulliken Oak, 38.
Munroe, Marrett, 17, 18.
Munroe Tavern, 28, 32.
Munroe, Wm., 15.
Muzzey Homestead, 40.
" Muzzy, Nibour," 7, 13.
Mystic Lake, 65.

Natick, 69.
Nine-acre Corner, 69.
Normal School, 21, 22.
North Brook, 19, 40, 50, 54.
North Lexington, 51.
North St., 66.
Norumbega, 69.
Nutting's Pond, 68.

Oakland St., 53, 61.

Index.

Parker, Capt. John, 9, 14, 18, 19, 35.
Parker, Theodore, 14, 35, 65, 67.
Parker Pine, 36.
Peirce's Bridge, 66.
Percy, Earl, 28, 32.
Phinney, Elias, 36.
Pierce, Cyrus, 22.
Pierce Homestead, 43.
Pitcairn, Major, 27, 28, 58.
Pleasant St., 44, 64, 66.
Population, 5, 62.
Post offices, 14, 62, 72.
Powder House, 68.
Private Residences, 36, 38, 39, 41, 42, 46, 47, 49, 50, 51, 52.
Public Buildings, 57.
Punkatasset Hill, 69.
Putnam, Gen., 59.

Railroad Accommodations, 5.
Railroad Stations, 12, 51, 62, 66.
Rebellion, The, 11.
Reed, William, 51.
Reed's Mill, 66, 67.
Revere, Paul, 25.
Revere St., 50.
Revolution, The, 11, 16, 20, 59.
Riverside, 70.
Robbins' Hill, 69.
Royall House, 68.
Russell House, 41.

Sanderson House, 32.
Sandham, 58.
Sandy Pond, 66, 67.
Savings Bank, 59.
Schools, 8, 9, 10, 57, 60, 61.
Schoolhouse, First, 8, 9.
Schoolhouse, Hancock, 10, 57.
School-house Hill, 8.
Sewall House, 67.
Shade St., 67.
Shawsheen River, 40, 64.
Shooting Club, 62.
Sketch Map, 1775, 26.
Smith Elm, 46.
"Smith End," 46.
Societies, 61, 71.
Spot Pond, 69.
Spring St., 36, 65, 67.

Spy Pond, 65.
Statues, 58.
Stetson, Caleb, 21.
Stoneham, 69.
Stores, 62.
Sudbury, 69.
Sudbury River, 69.

Tablets, Historical, 13, 16, 27, 31, 33, 34, 59, 61, 64, 65.
Taverns, 6, 28, 32.
Tidd House, 50.
Tophet Swamp, 64.
Town Hall, 57, 60.
Trapelo Road, 64.
Tufts' College, 68.
Turkey Hill, 65.

Valleyfield Farm, 38.
Valuation, 5.
Village Hall, 60.
Vine Brook, 7, 39, 41, 66.
Virginia Road, 63.

Wachusett Mt., 5, 36.
Walden Pond, 67.
Walks, 63, 70.
Walnut St., 65.
Waltham, 53, 65, 67, 69.
Waltham St., 38, 39, 64, 65.
Washington, George, 32.
Watertown St., 66, 68.
Water-works, 55.
Waverly Oaks, 64.
Wayside Inn, 69.
Wellesley, 69.
Wellington, Benj., 44.
Wellington Elm, 42, 43.
Wellington Homestead, 44, 46.
Weston, 69.
Weston St., 64, 67, 69.
White Pond, 69.
"Willows," The, 65.
Winchester, 65, 69.
Woburn, 65, 66.
Woburn St., 41, 60, 66.
Wood St., 64, 68.
Women's Relief Corps, 62.
Wyman House, 67.

Zion's Hill, 65.

www.ingramcontent.com/pod-product-compliance
Lightning Source LLC
Chambersburg PA
CBHW020335090426
42735CB00009B/1549